LISTENING
FOR THE VOICE
OF GOD

LISTENING FOR THE VOICE OF GOD

GROWING IN FAITH EVERY DAY

Margaret Feinberg

Foreword by Marilyn Meberg

THOMAS NELSON
Since 1798

NASHVILLE   DALLAS   MEXICO CITY   RIO DE JANEIRO

Published in Nashville, Tennessee, by Thomas Nelson. Thomas Nelson is a registered trademark of Thomas Nelson, Inc.

Thomas Nelson, Inc., titles may be purchased in bulk for educational, business, fund-raising, or sales promotional use. For information, please e-mail SpecialMarkets@ThomasNelson.com.

Unless otherwise noted, Scripture quotations are taken from the NEW KING JAMES VERSION. © 1982 by Thomas Nelson, Inc. Used by permission. All rights reserved.

Scripture quotations marked NIV are taken from the HOLY BIBLE: NEW INTERNATIONAL VERSION®. © 1973, 1978, 1984 by International Bible Society. Used by permission of Zondervan Publishing House. All rights reserved.

ISBN: 978-1-4185-4405-8

Printed in China

14 15 16 17 DSC 13 12 11 10

Contents

Foreword   vii

Introduction: The Light for Our Paths   xi

Hearing God's Voice   1

1   God's Voice Creates   3

2   God's Voice Invites   9

3   God's Voice Exposes   15

4   God's Voice Surprises   21

The Ways God Speaks   27

5   God's Word as Foundation and Filter   29

6   God's Colorful Expressions   37

7   God's Personal Touch   43

8   God Whispers   49

The Wonder of God's Voice   55

9   God Calls Us to Know and Love Him   57

10 God Calls Us to Obedience   63

Contents

11 God Calls Us to Faith   69

12 God Calls Us to Wait   75

Leader's Guide   81

Notes   103

About the Author   105

Foreword

Imagine yourself in the checkout line at the grocery store. You over-hear a conversation between two women behind you: One woman asks the other, "What prompted you to shave off all of your hair?" The response you hear is, "God told me to." Might you wheel around and look at the woman with the shaved head to see if she looks as strange as her answer sounds? For a moment, you might give her the benefit of the doubt and think maybe she feels God encouraged her to shave her head because she is starting chemo treatment. Or, with an odd twist of bizarre logic, you might conclude that perhaps she tends to sweat during hot weather and thinks God empathizes and made a suggestion. Perhaps those rationales don't satisfy you so you look again to see if there is a hint of "crazy" in her eyes. The truth is when people say "God told me" or "I heard the voice of God," we often assume that person is unbalanced and find ways to avoid them.

You know, the Old Testament is filled with unsettling behavior from people who claimed to have heard the voice of God. Noah was told to build a boat in the desert to avoid a future and unprecedented flood. Moses heard from a burning bush that he was to deliver the Israelites from the tyranny of slavery in Egypt. Mary, the mother of Jesus, was told she carried the prophesied Messiah in her womb. Angels told shepherds to hurry off to Bethlehem, where they would find the newborn Messiah lying in a manger, of all places. These audible instructions don't seem as outlandish to us now because we know the outcome. There was indeed a devastating flood; Moses did lead the Israelites to God's promised land; Jesus, the Messiah, was born to Mary; and the shepherds discovered Jesus in a humble stable in Bethlehem.

But for us twenty-first-century women, who don't receive instruction from burning bushes or bright stars, how does God communicate to us? How do we know what He wants us to do? When we want to do the right thing, make godly decisions, and He's not talking out loud, how do we avoid mistakes? Can we miss His voice and mess up His plan? Those anxieties cause our heads to sweat.

You are holding in your hands a wonderfully balanced Bible study titled *Listening for the Voice of God*. Though we no longer have the advantage of hearing an audible voice from God, this study teaches us the many ways God communicates with us through His Holy and inspired Words: the Bible.

For example, one of the ways God communicates to me through Scripture is to remind me of the brilliant truth found in Romans 12:2: Let God transform you into a new person by changing the way you think. This message from God is huge; it covers everything. If I think negatively and have no confidence that God is working in my life, I am missing His encouraging voice to work on changing the way I think. The way I think is influenced by the study of Scripture as I read how God has consistently worked in the lives of His people throughout the ages. I am one of His people. He will work in my life too. I need to believe that and act upon it.

This study also discusses the kinds of voices God uses for us today. My favorite and most frequently experienced is His "quiet nudging" within my spirit. Often I feel a nudge that I can't deny. I know I am not imagining it, so where did the nudge come from? When I realize the nudge may be God's voice, I quit excusing it, fighting it, or ignoring it. God is speaking to me. Wow! I don't share that in the grocery checkout line, but I tune in and listen.

You are going to find your mind and spirit enlarged as you work your way through this study. And, if you are using this as a study for a group, you are going to experience a sweet kinship with one another. Learning and growing in the company of others is one of my favorite experiences. If you are feeling the "nudge," maybe you need to grab this study and start a group. I'm just sayin' . . .

—MARILYN MEBERG

Introduction

The Light for Our Paths

*Peace on the outside comes from
knowing God on the inside.*

AUTHOR UNKNOWN

Life is filled with countless decisions, options, and opportunities. We face laundry lists of questions every day about our work, our families, and our faith journeys.

Every woman has grappled with questions like "How do I know if I'm following God's plan for my life?" or "What does God want me to do in this situation?" Whenever we face challenges, struggles, or important decisions, our first place to turn is to God. But who hasn't struggled to discern God's voice just when we need it most?

God's Word tells us that He is a lamp to our feet and light for our paths, but lamps often only illuminate our next step forward. When one of life's storms blows through, it can feel as though we're alone in the dark—desperately needing God to make Himself real and show us where to go. On calmer, well-lit days we may try to run ahead of God and do things on our own.

What does it mean to slow down, wait on God, and hear His voice through the darker and brighter spots in life? How can we walk with peace and confidence down the path God has for us no matter where it leads? What does it look like to have a vibrant relationship with God?

My hope and prayer is that through this study you'll begin discovering God's presence and voice in a fresh way. That as you get to know God and His Word, you'll walk with joy into everything He has for you.

Blessings,

Margaret Feinberg

Hearing God's Voice

Why is God's voice so important? This section will examine the nature of God's voice and its effect on our lives, which is more amazing than you can imagine.

One

God's Voice Creates

*People see God every day, they
just don't recognize him.*

Pearl Bailey,
American actress and singer

The first chapter of Genesis tells the story of creation. On each of the seven days, God was the Master Designer and Artist. He formed the cosmos, including our planet. He created oceans and seas and lakes and rivers and streams. He covered the land with vegetation, including trees and shrubs and flowers and berries. He filled the water with indescribable sea life, and the air with birds. Livestock and wild animals began exploring the land. On the sixth day, God created mankind, and on the seventh God rested.

One of the greatest wonders of the story of creation is that God created with mere words. When God said, "Let there be light," radiance flooded the earth. When He said, "Let the water teem with living creatures," sea life erupted in the depths of the ocean. With syllables, God spoke and creation happened. While we often think about all the plants and animals that God created, it's easy to forget that He also introduced incredible smells and textures and colors into our world. Creation was filled with a celebration of life and beauty.

Though theologians have long debated the interpretation of the first chapter of Genesis, there are some things that are easy to agree on, namely that the story of creation establishes God's power, majesty, and wisdom as the Creator. The hero of creation is God, and through the sound of His voice, He is intimately connected with all of creation.

The creation story is a potent reminder of the power of God's voice in our lives. When God finished creating the heavens and the earth, everything was teeming with life. And when we encounter God's voice in our lives, we can't help teeming with a renewed sense of the life God wants to give us. God's voice gives us the courage to overcome our fears, grow in our faith journeys, and become whom God has created us to be.

> *God's voice gives us the courage to overcome our fears, grow in our faith journeys, and become whom God has created us to be.*

1. *Have you ever encountered God's presence or voice in your life? Describe the experience.*

2. What are some of the primary ways God speaks to you? Are there any particular things that God tends to use to get your attention?

3. Read **Genesis 1**. If you could pick one of the seven days described in the creation story to watch God at work, which one would you choose? Why?

4. Reflecting on **Genesis 1**, what surprises you most about the creation story? What does this passage reveal about God and His involvement in our world? Our lives?

The story of creation is referred to throughout the Bible. It's even mentioned when the Ten Commandments were given to Moses on Mount Sinai.

5. Read *Exodus 20:1–21*. *Which commandment refers to the creation story (vv. 8–11)? Why do you think God chose to do what He did on the seventh day of creation?*

6. *How did God display His power in this passage (vv. 18–19)? Do you think this display reminded the people that God was their all-powerful Creator? Why or why not?*

7. *Throughout the Bible, we are reminded of God as the Creator. Look up the following verses and write down what God created in each one.*

   Nehemiah 9:6:

   Psalm 24:1–2:

   Psalm 33:6:

8. *How does knowing that God is our Creator and that He has incredible power in His words affect the way you respond to His voice in your life?*

> **With mere words God spoke our world and all its wonders into existence. When God speaks to you and me, He is speaking life, hope, and a future.**

Digging Deeper

In Genesis 1 the Scripture says, God "made" five times. Six times the writer described something that God saw was "good" (vv. 4, 10, 12, 18, 21, 25). Read **Genesis 1:31.** What did God think of what He made on this day? Why do you think the writer described it in this way?

God looked at what He had created and concluded that it was very good. Is it easy or hard for you to look on other people who God has created and see them as good? What about when you look at yourself? Do you see that what God has done in creating you is good? Explain.

Bonus Activity

Go online this week or spend some time searching through magazines to find the most beautiful portrait of God's creation that you can find. At the next gathering, bring in a copy of your artwork. It may be an image printed from a Web site, a magazine article, or something else that captures the wonder of nature. Share it with the group, and discuss the amazing power of God in our world.

Two

God's Voice Invites

Every evening I turn my worries over to God.
He's going to be up all night anyway.

MARY CROWLEY,
AUTHOR AND FOUNDER OF HOME INTERIORS AND GIFTS

The stars filled the sky like glitter spread across a black canvas. The three men sat in awe as they rode their horses through the Colorado night. As they followed the rugged trail along the base of the mountain, a voice in the distance commanded them to stop and dismount. Startled by the mysterious command, they obeyed without hesitation.

"Walk to the riverbed and pick up some pebbles," the voice instructed. "Place them in your backpacks, but do not look at them until morning."

The men struggled to stand on the slippery rocks that lined the raging river. Finding footholds among the crevices, they each reached down, scooping up a handful of small stones. Looking around, they saw no one. They heard no one. They returned to their horses.

They were about to signal to the animals that it was time to move on when the mysterious voice returned, "This will be both the happiest and saddest day of your lives." The men looked at one another in the faint moonlight. What could this mean?

At the first shadows of sunrise, the men reached for their saddlebags. To their delight, the pebbles they had gathered the night before turned to gold. They laughed with joy. They had found unexpected treasure.

"But what do you think the voice meant that this would be the saddest day of our lives?" one of the men asked. "Is something bad going to happen?"

"It already has," one of the men explained. "Yes, we have gold, but think how rich we would be if only we had picked up more."

The Creator of the universe, the One who fashioned the world, desires a personal relationship with each of us.

This story illustrates that sometimes we can go through life, circumstances, and specific events and not recognize the incredible opportunity we've been given. We may pass by or not lay hold of the fullest of the amazing possibilities that are before us. This isn't only true in everyday life; it's also true in our relationship with God.

The Creator of the universe, the One who fashioned the world, desires a personal relationship with each of us. He doesn't just want to be part of our lives; He wants to be the center of our lives—the foundation of everything we are. He wants to fill us with His love, empower us with His strength, and infuse us with His hope. God's voice invites us into an adventure that's wilder than we could have imagined, and in the process He gives us more than we could ever ask for or expect.

1. *Imagine that you're riding a horse in the middle of the night and a voice instructs you to take a handful of pebbles from a nearby stream. Would your instinct be to take a lot of pebbles or a few? Why?*

2. *Now imagine that you're standing before God and He says, "I will give you what you ask for." Would you tend to ask God for a little or a lot? Why? What specifically would you ask God for?*

The idea of standing before God and being able to ask for anything may sound strange, but that's exactly what prayer is. Prayer is the ability to come before God at any time and share your wants, needs, desires, hopes, dreams, and your very self with Him. Prayer is simply an open and honest dialogue between you and the Creator of the universe.

3. *Read* **Matthew 7:7–11**. *Why do you think Jesus invited us to pray? What promises did Jesus give to us if we pray? What does this passage reveal about the nature of God?*

The invitation to pray is given to us each and every day. Throughout the Bible, we see men and women responding to the invitation to express their voices to God and listen to God's voice. People pray in different ways.

4. *Consider the different postures people have during prayer. Look up the following passages. What posture does each person take as he or she prays and communicates with God?*

Genesis 24:26:

Numbers 20:6:

1 Kings 8:22:

1 Kings 8:54:

Though we may answer the invitation to pray, there are times when we all struggle to find the right words to say what we're really thinking and feeling in our hearts.

5. Read **Romans 8:26–27**. What does this passage reveal about the Holy Spirit's role in our prayer life? How have you found this to be true in your own spiritual journey?

6. All of our prayers will look and sound different. The important thing is that we are answering the invitation to pray. Look up the following passages. What is being asked for in the prayer?

Scripture Reference	What Is Being Asked for in the Prayer?
Genesis 18:23–26	
Genesis 32:24–26	
Daniel 9:4–6, 17–19	
Matthew 6:11	
Ephesians 3:14–19	

7. Which of these passages encourages you the most in your own prayer life?

8. *In what ways do you sense God inviting you to connect with Him more often? Where in your schedule and the busyness of life can you take time to pray?*

> *God's voice invites us into a deeper relationship with Him through prayer. If we want to hear God's voice, then we need to take advantage of this golden opportunity to seek and know Him.*

Digging Deeper

Read 2 Chronicles 7:14. Why is humility important when it comes to prayer and seeking God? What does God promise to those who humble themselves, pray, and turn from their ways? In what ways have you found this passage to be true in your own life?

Bonus Activity

On a blank sheet of paper, make a list of things that prevent you from answering the invitation to pray and hear God's voice. Spend some time in quiet reflection. Then offer up each one of the concerns to God in prayer. Ask Him to begin removing any obstacles in your life. At the end of your reflective time, crumple up the sheet of paper and throw it away as a sign that the things listed are going to be removed as obstacles in your life.

Three

God's Voice Exposes

*The relationship between God and a man is
more private and intimate than any possible
relation between two fellow creatures.*

C. S. LEWIS,
BRITISH AUTHOR AND APOLOGIST

Did you know that if you go to Washington, D.C., you can visit
the International Spy Museum? It is the first public museum in the
United States to provide an insider's look at the secretive profession
of spying. Throughout the museum, visitors encounter the stories of
spies, told through exhibits and film, and explore how espionage has
affected historic as well as current events.

The museum features the largest collection of international spy-
related gadgets and gizmos ever displayed publicly. You'll find that
buttonhole cameras, invisible ink, and submarine recording systems
aren't just the stuff of great movies; they're really used by spies! If
you love whodunits or detective shows, you'll probably be intrigued
by the museum's look at the game of spying.[1]

While the art of spying may stir our imaginations and pique our interest, God's knowledge of us and our world does not depend on the shadowy realm of intrigue and espionage. God doesn't need a hidden camera or a disguise to know what's going on in our lives. He sees everything. He knows everything. And He wants to bring everything that is hidden to the light.

In **Matthew 10:26–31** Jesus instructed:

Therefore do not fear them. For there is nothing covered that will not be revealed, and hidden that will not be known.

Whatever I tell you in the dark, speak in the light; and what you hear in the ear, preach on the housetops. And do not fear those who kill the body but cannot kill the soul. But rather fear Him who is able to destroy both soul and body in hell. Are not two sparrows sold for a copper coin? And not one of them falls to the ground apart from your Father's will. But the very hairs of your head are all numbered. Do not fear therefore; you are of more value than many sparrows.

God doesn't need a hidden camera or a disguise to know what's going on in our lives. He sees everything. He knows everything. And He wants to bring everything that is hidden to the light.

We serve a God who is all-powerful and all-knowing. Just as a sparrow does not fall from the sky without God noticing, neither does a hair fall from your head. God knows. He sees our motives and our innermost thoughts. Furthermore, when God speaks, His words expose. They reveal things about ourselves that we could not know on our own. He knows far more than any spy ever could.

1. *What are some of your favorite spy and detective shows, books, and movies?*

2. *What aspects of a spy or detective story do you enjoy the most (for example, guessing who the criminal is, watching the detectives, sorting through the evidence)? What, to you, makes a great spy or detective story?*

The words God speaks often expose our own hearts. While most of us have never heard the audible voice of God, we have had a sense in our hearts when something isn't quite right, a gnawing impression that we've done something or someone wrong. That quiet nudging is God's voice. Sometimes that sense of conviction that something isn't quite right challenges us to go back and apologize to someone, to be fully honest, or to acknowledge our own mistakes. It exposes something in us. The wondrous part of this experience is that when God's voice exposes something in our hearts, it is to bring us to wholeness in our relationship with Him and others—if we will listen to Him.

3. Read **Genesis 4:1–15**. Why was Cain so upset (vv. 3–5)?

4. What did the Lord say to Cain (vv. 6–7)? How did the Lord's words reveal what was going on in Cain's heart and how he should respond? What did Cain choose to do (v. 8)?

5. Have you ever been in a situation where, like Cain, you felt God asking you to let go of your pride? How did you respond?

In the Old Testament, King David wanted to build a temple for God, but instead, Solomon, his son, was chosen to do it.

6. *Read* **1 Chronicles 28:1–9**. *Why did God not allow David to build the temple (v. 3)?*

7. *Read* **1 Chronicles 28:9–21**. *What practical instruction did David give to Solomon for building the temple (vv. 11–19)? What spiritual instruction did David give him (vv. 9–10, 20–21)? Do you think Solomon needed to hear these spiritual instructions? Why or why not?*

8. *David gave Solomon valuable spiritual wisdom and instruction that he knew his son would need. What valuable spiritual wisdom and instruction have you been given that has changed your heart, life, or perspective?*

When God's voice exposes something in our hearts, it's to bring us to wholeness in our relationship with Him and others—if we will listen to Him.

Digging Deeper

Read Jesus' words to His disciples in **John 14–17**. Is there anything about the words of Jesus that surprise you? Anything that is particularly meaningful? Anything that exposes something in your own heart right now? Explain.

Bonus Activity

King David is described as having a heart after God's. David was not afraid to expose his heart to God in honest worship and prayer and have God expose the truth of who He is to David. Over the next week, read a psalm a day and reflect on the author's honesty before God, and God's honest response.

Four

God's Voice Surprises

Faith is believing in things when
common sense tells you not to.

GEORGE SEATON,
AMERICAN SCREENWRITER AND DIRECTOR

Have you ever felt as though you're not a first-round draft selection when it comes to being used by God? Have you ever felt that there are other choices that just make more sense? People who are smarter, better looking, or more gifted?

If so, you are not alone! At times, we all feel hints of insecurity and self-doubt. But when God looks at us, He doesn't focus on what we can't do; He sees what He can do through us. In fact, sometimes the individual whom God chooses can be surprising—not only to us but also to the one chosen.

Consider Moses. He had a profound encounter with God in Exodus 3 in which God chose him to lead the Israelites out of Egypt and into the freedom God had for them. Moses didn't throw his hand up in the air and say, "I'm here and ready to go!" Instead, he argued with God, offering up a laundry list of weaknesses and doubts.

Moses reminded God that he had a speech impediment and couldn't speak in public very well. He was not a confident leader. Yet God saw past Moses' anxieties and knew that he was the best choice. No one was probably more surprised than Moses himself.

Another example is Jeremiah. When God came to Jeremiah and spoke to him, appointing him as a prophet to the nations, Jeremiah was surprised. His immediate concern was that he didn't know how to speak, and he was so young that no one would listen to him. But the Lord reminded Jeremiah not to allow his youth or insecurities to get the best of him. Instead, Jeremiah was to obey God with courage.

When God looks at us, He doesn't focus on what we can't do; He sees what He can do through us.

God has an amazing way of surprising us with what He's asking us to us do! Throughout the Bible we read of men and women who saved nations, led thousands to freedom, performed miracles, and followed Jesus to their own deaths. All were surprised by what God had called them to, but they still chose to answer the call.

Though you may not feel as if you're the obvious choice for honoring God with your life, no one qualifies according to their own merit. God uses a responsive and willing heart to do amazing things.

1. *Do you tend to think that God calls the qualified, or that He qualifies the called? Explain.*

2. *What is something that you felt God was calling you to that seemed impossible or bigger than yourself? How did you respond? What was the result?*

First Samuel 3 records the Lord calling to Samuel as a young boy. Samuel's response launched him into a remarkable journey of serving and obeying God.

3. *Read **1 Samuel 3**. In this passage, whom do you think was the most surprised that God spoke to Samuel? What was Samuel's response to God's voice? In what ways should our response to God's voice be similar to Samuel's?*

Like Samuel, Isaiah also had a profound encounter with God that changed the course of his life.

4. *Read **Isaiah 6**. What did Isaiah see and experience with God in this passage?*

While many people in the Bible had profound encounters with God, others had encounters with God simply because they chose to follow Jesus and obey Him. In John 1, we read of Jesus calling some of His disciples.

5. Read **John 1:35–51**. *What are some of the different ways Jesus revealed Himself to the disciples and invited them to follow Him?*

6. *Which of the disciples' stories of meeting Jesus most parallels your own?*

7. *What are some ways in your own life that God's voice has surprised you?*

8. What would it look like for you to have a more ready and willing ear to respond to God's surprising voice in your life?

> When you're listening for God, you can expect the unexpected. God's voice has a way of surprising us and catching us off guard. God has more to say to you than you ever imagined.

Digging Deeper

Like Isaiah's call, Jeremiah's encounter with God was extraordinary. Read **Jeremiah 1**. Why do you think God met with Jeremiah in this way? Why do you think God chooses to meet people in such diverse ways? How has God met you in the past? How is this different from the ways God meets other people you know?

Bonus Activity

Take a moment and imagine that your heart is a house with many rooms—multiple bedrooms, bathrooms, and even a sitting area. To which rooms of your house does God have access? God wants to be welcome into your whole house, your whole heart. In **Revelation 3:20** (NIV) God says, "Here I am! I stand at the door and knock. If anyone hears my voice and opens the door, I will come in and eat with him, and he with me." Spend some time prayerfully reflecting on any areas of your heart and life to which you have not given God access, and invite Him in.

The Ways God Speaks

God speaks in many different ways,

often unexpectedly, in order to

communicate His heart to us.

Five

God's Word
as Foundation and Filter

*I have found in the Bible words for my inmost
thoughts, songs for my joy, utterance for my hidden
griefs and pleadings for my shame and feebleness.*

SAMUEL TAYLOR COLERIDGE,
ENGLISH POET AND PHILOSOPHER

Knowing the Bible is crucial to understanding and discerning God's
voice in our lives. The pages of Scripture are chock-full of God's
wonderful voice. In order to fully recognize and respond to God, we
must take advantage of the God-breathed words He left for us: the
Bible. Then we are able to use God's Word as a foundation and filter
for all that we think we're hearing from God.

Take the Bible Trivia Quick Quiz on the next page and tally your
score (one point per correct answer). See how much Bible knowledge you have tucked away. Use the Scripture references at the end
of each question for helpful hints.

Bible Trivia Quick Quiz:
Brushing Up on Your Scripture Knowledge

1. This woman was a prophetess and a judge leading Israel during the defeat of Sisera and Jabin's army. (Judges 4:4–23)

   a. Rebekah

   b. Jael

   c. Deborah

2. This man was part of the early Christian church and was stoned to death after proclaiming the truth of the power of God. (Acts 6:8–7:60)

   a. Peter

   b. Stephen

   c. Simon

3. Who said, "Lord, I am not worthy that You should come under my roof. But only speak a word, and my servant will be healed"? (see Matthew 8:5–13)

   a. Paul

   b. David

   c. A centurion (army officer or captain)

4. She was the cousin of Mary, aunt to Jesus, and mother to John the Baptist. (Luke 1:5–25)

   a. Mary Magdalene

   b. Elizabeth

   c. Ruth

5. He was a relative of Naomi and owned fields where Ruth gleaned. (Ruth 2:1–9)

   a. Boaz

   b. Laban

   c. Ishmael

6. Who said, "Let the words of my mouth and the meditation of my heart be acceptable in Your sight, O LORD, my strength and my Redeemer"? (Psalm 19:14)

   a. Saul

   b. Solomon

   c. David

7. Who said, "Do not be afraid, Abram. I am your shield, your exceedingly great reward"? (Genesis 15:1)

   a. Sarah

   b. God

   c. Lot

8. She was a prostitute who was passionately pursued by Hosea. (Hosea 1:1–3)

   a. Gomer

   b. Hannah

   c. Rahab

9. He was an author of one of the Gospels and also a doctor. (Colossians 4:14)

   a. Luke

   b. John

   c. Mark

10. *Who said, "Sir, You have nothing to draw with, and the well is deep. Where then do You get that living water? Are You greater than our father Jacob, who gave us the well, and drank from it himself, as well as his sons and his livestock?"? (John 4:1–26)*

a. *Mary*

b. *Samaritan woman*

c. *crippled woman*

See the Leader's Guide in the back for answers.

Scoring

> *Even those who read the Bible their entire lives discover that there's still more to learn. That's part of the wonder of the Bible—as much as you know, there's always more to discover.*

If you answered **6–10** correctly, you've probably been studying the Bible for years. You're familiar with the stories, you recognize the quotes, and you have a handle on where to find stories in the Scriptures.

If you answered **0–5** correctly, you may be new to studying and reading the Scriptures. No worries—even those who read the Bible their entire lives discover that there's still more to learn. That's part of the wonder of the Bible—as much as you know, there's always more to discover.

Regardless of your score on the quiz, God's Word is meant to be treasured in our hearts. The people in the pages of Scripture were all created and known by God. He encountered them and spoke to them in various ways. As we study the Bible, the stories and passages expand the spiritual library that the Holy Spirit can use to speak to us and draw our hearts back to God's own.

1. *What was the most challenging aspect of the Bible Trivia Quick Quiz? Is it easy or hard for you to remember the details of what you read in the Bible? Explain.*

2. *On a scale from 1 to 10, how much do you enjoy reading and studying Scripture? Explain your choice.*

(**Least Enjoy**) 1–2–3–4–5–6–7–8–9–10 (*Most Enjoy*)

Scripture is God's love letter to us. As we study and get to know God's Word, we are better able to discern His voice from the other voices we encounter in our lives. Jesus experienced this truth first-hand in the Gospel of Matthew. When He went out to the desert, the tempter tried to convince Jesus to do several things. Jesus stood firmly against temptation by quoting God's Word.

3. *Read **Matthew 4:1–11**. What did the tempter first tell Jesus to do (v. 3)? What was Jesus' response (v. 4)?*

4. What was the second temptation from the devil (v. 6)? What was Jesus' response (v. 7)?

5. What was the third temptation that the devil offered (v. 9)? What was Jesus' reply (v. 10)? What is the significance of Jesus quoting an Old Testament passage?

6. Look up the following verses, and describe what they reveal about God's Word.

Scripture Reference	What Is Revealed about God's Word?
Psalm 119:89	
Isaiah 40:8	
Matthew 5:18	
Psalm 119:11	

7. *Have you ever had a time in your life when God's Word helped you avoid sinning or hurting yourself or someone else? Describe.*

8. *Why is God's Word so important in discerning whether what you're thinking is really from God or not?*

God's Word helps us discern whether or not what we're hearing is truly from God. By becoming familiar with Scripture, we are more equipped to detect God's voice in our lives.

Digging Deeper

Read 2 Timothy 3:16–17. In this passage, Paul encouraged and instructed his young mentee, Timothy. Fill in the chart on the next page, explaining how God's Word has been a source of teaching, rebuking, correcting, and training in righteousness in your own life.

For What God's Word Is Useful	Observation in Your Life
Teaching	
Rebuking	
Correcting	
Training in righteousness	

Bonus Activity

Every day in the upcoming week, set aside time to read Scripture. Choose a particular character to study all week, or select a book of the Bible to focus on, such as 1 John. Before you read, take time to ask God for clarity and understanding. Share what you learn with a friend.

Six

God's Colorful Expressions

*Whenever I see sunbeams coming through
clouds, it always looks to me like God shining
himself down onto us. The thing about
sunbeams is they're always there even though
we can't always see them. Same with God.*

ADELINE CULLEN RAY,
AUTHOR

You simply can't put God in a box. God has a way of expressing Himself in surprising ways throughout Scripture. From the very beginning in Genesis, God communicated with Adam and Eve. But even after a willful act of disobedience that forced Adam and Eve to leave the garden, God continued to speak to His people. God warned Cain not to allow his anger to get the best of him (Genesis 4:6–7), God instructed Noah to build a big boat because a rainstorm was on its way (Genesis 6:13–21), and God promised Abram that he would have many children even though his wife was infertile (Genesis 12, 15, 17–18).

God used colorful ways to communicate to His people throughout the Bible. In Exodus 3, Moses encountered and heard from God in the form of a burning bush. God spoke to some people through dreams. One of the most famous dreamers of the Bible is Joseph. As a teenager, he had a dream that he was going to be greater than his brothers. He foolishly told them about the dream, and they were angry at him for it. Joseph's story is full of loss, heartache, imprisonment, wrongful accusations, and pain. Yet the dream God gave Joseph still came true.

Though we may be tempted to try to put God and His voice in a box . . . God will go to great lengths to communicate with us.

One unusual way that God speaks to His people in the Bible is through visions. Some of God's people actually saw images that were from God. Both Ezekiel and Daniel received visions from God, recorded in the Old Testament, and Paul and John received them and recorded them in the New Testament.

God also speaks through miracles. When the Israelites found themselves pinned up against the Red Sea with the Egyptian armies rushing toward them and nowhere to go, God opened up the Red Sea as a display of His power and love (Exodus 14). God often used angels throughout the Bible to communicate His heart to His people. In Luke 1, an angel delivered the incredible news of the birth of Jesus.

Indeed, God speaks through His Word (2 Timothy 3:16) and through the inner, still, small voice of the Holy Spirit (Acts 11:12; 13:2). God uses colorful and unexpected ways to speak into our lives. Though we may be tempted to try to put God and His voice in a box, Scripture reminds us that God will go to great and amazing lengths to communicate with each of us.

1. *Has God ever surprised you by communicating to you in an unusual way? Describe.*

2. *On the list below, place a check mark by any of the ways you feel God has communicated with you.*

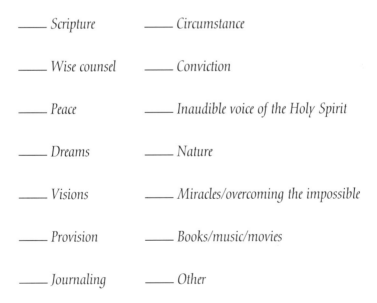

_____ *Scripture*   _____ *Circumstance*

_____ *Wise counsel*   _____ *Conviction*

_____ *Peace*   _____ *Inaudible voice of the Holy Spirit*

_____ *Dreams*   _____ *Nature*

_____ *Visions*   _____ *Miracles/overcoming the impossible*

_____ *Provision*   _____ *Books/music/movies*

_____ *Journaling*   _____ *Other*

3. *Reflecting on the list on page 39, are there any ways in which God has not spoken to you that you wish He would? Describe.*

4. *Why do you think God uses so many different ways to communicate His heart to His people?*

One of the reasons God communicates to us in such colorful ways is that His ways are different from our own. Because He is all-knowing and all-powerful, God has a different perspective.

5. *Read **Isaiah 55:8–9**. How are God's thoughts and ways different from our own?*

Despite the fact that God has a different perspective, He doesn't keep it from us. In His love, He wants to communicate to us, to lead us, and to guide us.

6. *Read 1 Corinthians 2. What is the source of knowing God and His wisdom?*

First Corinthians 2 tells us that "no eye has seen, no ear has heard, no mind has conceived" (v. 9 NIV) all that God has for us. Yet God wants to reveal these things to us.

7. *Why is hearing from God essential to knowing what God has for you? Are there any areas of your life where you are asking God to reveal what He has for you? As you wait for the answer, what comfort do you find in this passage?*

8. *If you could ask God one question and receive an answer right away, what would you ask Him?*

> *God reveals Himself in colorful ways throughout the Scripture and in our lives through His Spirit.*

Digging Deeper

Read **Revelation 1:9–10.** What did God's voice sound like to John? Has God's voice ever sounded loud and blaring like a trumpet to you? Why do you think God chooses to speak loud and clear sometimes, and other times He is more difficult to hear?

Bonus Activity

Each day this week, spend some time asking God to speak to you. Ask Him to give you eyes to see the ways He is moving in your life, ears to hear the ways He is speaking, and a heart that is ready to respond to His leading. Be expectant for the colorful ways God may reveal Himself to you.

Seven

God's Personal Touch

Faith is like radar that sees through the fog the reality of things at a distance that the human eye cannot see.

CORRIE TEN BOOM,
HOLOCAUST SURVIVOR AND AUTHOR OF *THE HIDING PLACE*

God is the source of our hope, strength, and peace. He has a way of making Himself real to us in the most personal ways and at the most needed times.

In 1929, legendary retailer J. C. Penney became severely ill. Hospitalized in Battle Creek, Michigan, his conditioned worsened. Hope slipped away. One evening he decided to write farewell notes to his family. He doubted he would make it through the night, and he wanted them to know of his love for them.

To his surprise, Penney made it through the night. The next morning he managed to climb out of bed and make his way down to the chapel where devotions were held each morning. As he made his way down the hallway, he recognized the hymn "God Will Take Care of You." He quietly crept into the service. Though his heart and body were exhausted and spent, something incredible happened. Describing the moment, Penney said, "I felt as if I had been instantly lifted out of the darkness of a dungeon into a warm, brilliant sunlight. I felt as if I had been transported from hell to paradise."[1]

Penney described feeling the power of God as he had never felt it before. In His love, God was there in a real and tangible way to help him.

> *No matter what situation we find ourselves in, God has a way of meeting us there.*

Like J. C. Penney, many of us find ourselves, at one time or another, overwhelmed and losing hope. We may wonder where God is in the middle of our situation. But like Penney, we may discover that God is closer and more involved than we ever imagined. Not only did Penney awake with the strength to make it to the chapel, but the words of the hymn the congregation sang were personally meaningful to him. They spoke right into his situation. And in the midst of the chapel service, God met J. C. Penney in a profound way.

No matter what situation we find ourselves in, God has a way of meeting us there. He may use songs, prayers, a sermon, an encouraging word from a friend, or something even more surprising to speak right into our situation at the place of our greatest need. When it comes to caring for you, God makes it personal.

1. Have you ever had God meet you at a critical time in a personal way? Describe the event.

2. Has God ever used a song or hymn to speak to you or encourage you? If so, what was the song and what was the situation?

3. Why do you think God communicates to us in such personal ways—specific ways that speak directly into our situation, our personalities, and our experiences?

Following Jesus' death, resurrection, and reappearance, the disciples gathered as Jesus instructed them to and waited for God. The Holy Spirit came on this gathering of followers in a profound way, and many became Christians or followers of Christ. This upset the Jewish rulers, and opposition followed. Stephen, one of the believers in Jesus, was actually stoned to death for his beliefs.

4. Read Acts 7. What did Stephen tell the Sanhedrin (vv. 2–51)? How did the people respond to Stephen's defense of his faith (vv. 54–59)?

5. *Acts 8:1 is a small but profound verse. According to this passage, who was watching Stephen's stoning? What was this person's response?*

We find out why Acts 8:1 is important in Acts 9. The man who watched Stephen's death was about to have a profound and personal encounter with God.

6. *Read Acts 9:1–9. Why do you think that of all the ways that God could have encountered Saul, He did it in this way?*

7. *After Saul's miraculous blinding experience, God could have miraculously healed him on His own, but God chose to use Ananias. Read Acts 9:10–19. Why do you think Ananias was used to heal Saul? What effect do you think this had on Saul's spiritual outlook and life?*

8. *When it comes to speaking to His people, God will often use others to encourage us, help us, and even heal us in different ways. In what ways have you seen God use friends, family members, and even your community to help direct and lead you?*

> *Sometimes God makes Himself real in ways we don't even expect—but that are highly personal and incredibly meaningful to us.*

Digging Deeper

When you pray, do you wait with anticipation that God will answer? Read **Psalm 5:1–3**. According to this passage, when did the psalmist pray? What is the attitude of the psalmist toward God and answered prayer? What is your own attitude toward God and prayer when you pray? What can you do today to lay your requests before God and wait in expectation?

Bonus Activity

Choose one chapter of the Bible and write it out on a piece of paper each day this week. You may want to select a psalm or a chapter from the New Testament. As you write each verse, spend time prayerfully considering what the passage is saying and what God may want to speak to you through it.

Eight

God Whispers

*The self-appointed spokesmen for God incline to
shout; He, Himself, speaks only in whispers.*

MARTIN H. FISCHER,
AUTHOR AND PHYSICIAN

Elijah ran hard and fast. Fearing the threat of Jezebel, he knew he
had to get out of Israel. "May the gods deal with me, be it ever so
severely, if by this time tomorrow I do not make your life like that of
one of them" (1 Kings 19:2 NIV). Jezebel's words haunted him every
step of the way. She was referring to the pagan prophets whom, with
the help of God, Elijah had defeated on top of Mount Carmel.

Elijah sprinted hard to the point of exhaustion. He felt the tired-
ness in his muscles, his body, and his spirit. Finally, he collapsed
beneath a desert shrub. Without hope, he wanted to die. In fact,
he begged God to take his life. Even death seemed better than the
loneliness and fatigue that came from living on the run from the evil
Jezebel. Hopelessly, he fell asleep.

When Elijah awoke, he was greeted by an angel, who fed him
bread and gave him water. The humble meal gave Elijah the strength

he needed to keep going. Infused with hope and the power of God, Elijah had enough sustenance to travel the forty days to Horeb, also known as the mountain of God. This was the same mountain where Moses had met God many years before.

When you whisper to a friend, you have to lean in and get close. When God whispers to us, it's an invitation to lean in to our relationship with Him.

Tucked away in a cave, Elijah heard the voice of God ask, "What are you doing here, Elijah?"

Elijah exploded with honesty. He figured he had nothing to lose, so why not be completely honest with God? He recounted recent events: his attack on the false prophets and Jezebel's death threats. God didn't answer a single one of Elijah's concerns. Instead, the Lord commanded Elijah to go to the mountainside and wait for Him to pass by.

As Eljiah waited on God, a powerful, loud wind tore at the mountains, breaking branches and crushing rocks. But the Lord was not in the wind.

Then a terrifying earthquake shook the whole mountain, causing rocks to fall. But the Lord was not in the earthquake.

Then a horrifying fire swept the mountainside, devouring everything in its path. But the Lord was not in the fire.

Then Elijah heard a gentle whisper. The Lord was in this whisper—speaking through the sheer silence, and capturing Elijah's attention.

Just like Elijah in 1 Kings 19, we all feel frail and weak against our enemies. Like Elijah, we have days when we feel as though we're at the end of our rope and ready to let go. But even in those moments, God is on our side. He wants to speak to us. Though we may desire God to speak through earthshaking moments or thunderous sounds, often He communicates through much gentler means.

When we want to hear from God, we may be expecting to hear His voice come loudly and powerfully, but God frequently speaks in a whisper. One reason for this may be that it invites us into a closer relationship with Him. When you whisper to a friend, you have to lean in and get close. When God whispers to us, it's an invitation to lean in to our relationship with Him, to get even closer than we may have ever done in the past.

1. *Why do you think God chose to approach Elijah in the form of a whisper rather than the wind, earthquake, or fire?*

2. *Do you think the wind, earthquake, and fire prepared Elijah to hear from God? Why or why not?*

At this point in Elijah's spiritual journey, he had hit rock bottom. He felt afraid and defeated. He wanted to give up.

3. Read *1 Kings 19:1–9*. Have you ever had a time in your life when, like Elijah, you were ready to give up?

4. What gave you the strength to make it through that time?

5. Did you feel that God's presence during that challenging time was more like the wind, the earthquake, the fire, or the gentle whisper? Explain.

As the story in 1 Kings 19 progresses, it's interesting to note that Elijah had the exact same conversation with God twice. On two occasions God asked Elijah what he was doing in this place—after the angel had instructed him to go to that location. Each time Elijah answered God in the same way. It was only after the second time that God answered Elijah's concern differently.

6. Read *1 Kings 19:10–18*. What encouragement did God finally offer Elijah (vv. 15–18)?

In a moment in time, God met one of His prophets' needs on every level—spiritually, physically, emotionally, and relationally.

7. Reflecting on *1 Kings 19:1–18*, how did God meet Elijah in each of the following ways:

Spiritually:

Physically:

Emotionally:

Relationally:

8. *In your own times of need, how has God met you in each of these ways?*

Spiritually:

Physically:

Emotionally:

Relationally:

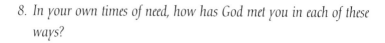

God wants to speak to us. He desires a relationship with us. God often gets our attention with subtle nudges.

Digging Deeper

Read **Hebrews 11:5–6.** What do you think Enoch's relationship with God was like? Why is faith so crucial to our journeys? In what ways are you seeking God in your daily life? What comfort have you found from God as you trust Him?

Bonus Activity

Go to your local library and check out a book on famous quotations and look up all the entries that discuss faith. Or consider going on-line and Googling "faith quotes." Pick your top three, write them on a note card, and bring them to the study the following week. Share your favorites with the other participants, and encourage one another with what you discover.

The Wonder of God's Voice

*Of all the things God will call you to
when you hear His voice, the greatest
thing He is calling you to is Himself.*

Nine

God Calls Us to Know and Love Him

Love him totally who gave himself
totally for you to love.

CLAIRE OF ASSISI,
ITALIAN SAINT

Mark Batterson is the pastor of National Community Church in Washington, D.C. As pastor of this growing congregation, he's faced many challenges. One of the biggest hurdles he faced early in the life of the church was the cost of real estate in the capital city. Unable to purchase a building, he decided to embrace an innovative solution: using theaters for people to gather on Sunday mornings. Today, countless churches around the country have embraced this model and use movie theaters as their meeting areas.

Batterson observes that while religion is focused on doing things for God, Christianity is all about receiving what Christ has done for us on the cross. Our response to God is merely a reflection of what God has already done for us. He describes how a few years ago he struggled with a tough season of discouragement. To get out of his spiritual slump, he decided to follow the advice of Revelation 2:5 and do the things he did in the beginning of his faith journey—he decided to take forty days to focus on God. During those five-and-a-half weeks, he spent extra time in prayer. He purchased a new Bible, and he read it cover to cover. In the process, he found himself leaving a season of life where God seemed distant and silent, entering one where God spoke to him through Scripture and everyday life.

Our response to God is merely a reflection of what God has already done for us.

One of the treasures of Batterson's season of pursuing God is something the Lord spoke to him during that time: It's not about what you can do for God; it's about what God has done for you.

That truth changed Batterson's life and has become a personal mantra for him. He recognizes that truly loving God is not about doing things for God, but receiving with thankfulness the things God has already done for us. At that point, we can reflect that love to others in our lives.[1]

God calls us to know Him and love Him. As we discover who God is—with all His wondrous attributes and characteristics—we can't help falling in love with Him and sharing that love with others we come in contact with.

1. *Have you ever taken time out of your busy schedule—for a partial day, full day, week, or longer—to focus on your relationship with God and reconnect with Him? What was the result? How were you changed or affected?*

2. What is your response to Mark Batterson's spiritual discovery, "It's not about what you can do for God; it's about what God has done for you"?

3. Do you find it easier to do things for God, or to reflect on all that God has done for you? Explain. Why is recognizing what God has done for you foundational to growing in your faith?

In the book of Revelation, an angel is described as writing seven different letters to the church. In the letter to the church of Ephesus, the angel commends this church for much of what they've done, but they are reminded of one thing they have forgotten.

4. Read **Revelation 2:1–7**. What was the church of Ephesus commended for? What was the angel's concern for the church of Ephesus?

5. *Think about when you first came to know and love God. What was your experience? How did you respond?*

All of us encounter and experience God in different ways. Some have dramatic encounters with God, while for others meeting God is much more subtle.

6. *Were there any things that you did in the beginning because of your love for God that you no longer do? Explain.*

Throughout the Bible we are encouraged not to lose heart when it comes to knowing, loving, and serving God. Though we face challenges, God is with us every step of the way.

7. *Read 2 Corinthians 4. In what ways does the image of treasures in jars of clay resonate with you?*

8. *What steps can you take to rekindle the passion for loving and knowing God in your own life?*

> *God invites us into a personal relationship with Him where we can grow in our faith. God loves us and calls us to love Him and express that love by loving others.*

Digging Deeper

Read **Psalm 95**. What does the psalmist say to glorify and celebrate God (vv. 1–6)? What does the psalmist say to challenge people in their faith journeys (vv. 7–8)? Are there any events in your life that have caused you to allow your heart to grow hard toward God or something He may want to say to you? What steps can you take to make yourself more ready and willing to hear God in your life?

Bonus Activity

Write down **2 Corinthians 4:7–12** on several note cards and place them around the house. Spend time memorizing and reciting this passage each day, and be encouraged that God is with you and loves you more than you can know.

Ten

God Calls Us to Obedience

*The strength and happiness of a man
consists in finding out the way in which
God is going, and going that way too.*

HENRY WARD BEECHER,
NINETEENTH-CENTURY CONGREGATIONALIST CLERGYMAN

As a Wycliffe missionary, Aretta Loving was familiar with living abroad. One morning, while she was washing breakfast dishes, she noticed her son, Jimmy, get up from the table and head toward the back porch.

Having just finished painting the handrails on the porch, she knew better than to send her five-year-old son out the back door. Instead she instructed her son to come around to the front door and explained that there was wet paint out back that he needed to avoid.

"I'll be careful!" Jimmy announced without turning around.

"No, Jimmy!" Loving protested. "Don't go that way."

"I'll be careful," Jimmy promised, nearing the back porch.

"Stop, Jimmy!" Loving shouted. "I don't want carefulness. I want obedience!"

Jimmy stopped, turned around, looked at his mother, and finally conceded. He headed toward the front door. As Loving watched her son make his way through the living room, she couldn't help wondering how many times she was like her own son, wanting only to go her own way. How many times had she rationalized and promised God that she'd be careful but still proceeded with her own plans?

> *Though God may speak a dozen or a hundred or even a thousand whispers into our hearts, what good is it if we do not obey?*

Though God may speak a dozen or a hundred or even a thousand whispers into our hearts, what good is it if we do not obey? God calls us to obedience and it's one of the greatest and most rewarding things we can be called to.

1. Like Jimmy in this story, have you ever been in a situation where you felt God telling you not to do something and you went ahead and did it anyway? What was the result?

2. Jimmy justified disobeying his mom by promising to be careful. When you are tempted to disobey something God has said to you, how do you justify it?

Saul was the first king of Israel, and he didn't recognize just how important obedience was to God. In 1 Samuel 15, Saul was rejected as king of Israel for his lack of obedience. The prophet Samuel instructed Saul to do specific things, but Saul justified doing what he wanted.

3. Read **1 Samuel 15:1–9**. What did Samuel specifically instruct Saul to do (vv. 1–3)?

4. What portion of Samuel's instructions did Saul obey? What portion did he not obey (vv. 7–9)?

5. Do you find complete disobedience or partial disobedience (as demonstrated by Saul) more tempting in your own life? Why?

When the prophet Samuel approached Saul about what happened, Saul defended his actions. In his own eyes, he hadn't done anything wrong. Yet Samuel explained that his lack of obedience was an expression of what was going on in Saul's heart.

6. Read *1 Samuel 15:10–21*. What were Saul's first words to Samuel when he saw the prophet after the battle (v. 13)? What were Samuel's first words to Saul (v. 14)?

7. How did Saul try to defend his actions (vv. 15, 20)?

8. Samuel's response cut to the heart of Saul's actions. Read *1 Samuel 15:22–23*. What are the heart issues behind Saul's disobedience? What heart issues often lurk behind our own disobedience?

God doesn't just invite us to know Him and love Him. We are also meant to obey Him as an expression of knowing and loving Him. Obedience is one of the greatest calls of God we can respond to in our lives.

Digging Deeper

In the Old Testament, the Israelites often disobeyed God. Read **Psalm 81:11–13**. What is the result of disobeying God? Why do you think God longs for us to walk in obedience? Why is God pleased with our obedience? What is one specific way in which you have obeyed God in the past week?

Bonus Activity

Spend some time in prayer this week. Is there one thing that God has been nudging you to do that you may have left undone? This may be something small, like calling a friend and offering an encouraging word, writing a note of thanks to someone meaningful, or sending a gift to someone you've meant to acknowledge. Whatever it might be, respond in obedience.

Eleven

God Calls Us to Faith

*Faith is taking the first step even when
you don't see the whole staircase.*

DR. MARTIN LUTHER KING JR.,
AMERICAN CIVIL RIGHTS LEADER

A young man decided to follow in his father's footsteps as a lumberjack. Full of vim and vigor, he was committed to chopping down more trees than any of the other men with whom he worked. As he headed to the job site, he set his heart, mind, and body on what he believed was an attainable goal: He wanted to chop down more trees than the company's average of fifteen per day.

His first day on the job, he managed to chop down ten trees. He realized that to reach his goal, he needed to work harder and smarter. He returned to the job site on the second day, committed to chopping down five more trees than the day before. But at the end of the day, he counted only ten. He hadn't made a bit of progress.

The third day he worked long and hard, but when he tallied the trees, he had chopped down only seven. Though puzzled and frustrated, he refused to give up. Maybe he was having an off day. The following day, he returned to the job but chopped down only five trees.

Each day his progress lessened. He experimented with changing the way he held the ax. He shifted his body position. He focused his mind. Yet at the end of each day, the number of trees that fell grew fewer and fewer. Several weeks passed. The discouraged young man approached a veteran lumberjack and explained that despite his best efforts, he was getting less done each day.

The grizzly lumberjack sized up the newcomer. Then he observed, "I see the calluses on your hands and the strength in your arms. I can tell you've been swinging your ax with everything you've got. But I can't help wondering, when was the last time you sharpened your ax?"[1]

> *"I can tell you've been swinging your ax with everything you've got. But I can't help wondering, when was the last time you sharpened your ax?"*

Like the lumberjack, we may feel that we're giving everything we have, but sometimes it doesn't feel as if we're getting anywhere. We need to remember that, like the lumberjack, we need to sharpen our spiritual axes. How? By remembering the promises God had made to us.

Though we may feel discouraged or worn down, God's Word is full of promises that sharpen us as followers of Jesus. God calls us to faith. He calls us to believe in Him and all that He can do in us and through us.

1. Are there any areas of your life where you feel as though you've been using a dull ax? If so, describe.

2. *What are some of the best ways that you use to sharpen the spiritual ax that helps you get through life?*

Though the disciples spent three years with Jesus and had the privilege of being with Him day in and day out, they still recognized the need for their faith to be increased and sharpened. In Luke 17, Jesus discusses the roles of faith, sin, and duty.

3. *Read **Luke 17:1–10**. Why do you think the disciples asked Jesus to increase their faith?*

In Ephesians 6, Paul challenges believers to put on the full armor of God.

4. Read **Ephesians 6:10–18**. Match up the pieces of armor for what they represent.

Pieces of Armor	Represents
Belt	
Breastplate	
Shoes	
Shield	
Helmet	
Sword	

5. According to this passage, what is the purpose of the shield of faith? How does faith serve as a shield in your own life?

Wherever Jesus went, He faced those who refused to believe He was the Son of God. The Jews persecuted Him at every turn. In John 5, Jesus healed a man on the Sabbath, and they found fault with Him.

6. Read **John 5:16–30.** How did Jesus defend Himself (vv. 19–23)?

7. What promise did Jesus offer in **John 5:24**? Have you accepted Jesus' promise for yourself? Why or why not?

8. What are some specific ways in which God is calling you to greater faith right now?

> *God invites us to trust Him wholly and choose to walk by faith. At times, we may be tempted to forget just how important faith is to our spiritual journeys, but it's essential to following God.*

Digging Deeper

Read Matthew 17:20. Why do you think Jesus made this promise to the disciples? Why is faith so important to God? To your own spiritual journey? When in your life have you been the most full of faith?

Bonus Activity

Make a list of three people for whom you really want to see God move in an active way. Pray for them every day this week. If you feel compelled, reach out to them in a loving way. Ask God to increase your faith as you pray for them, and trust Him to answer your prayers in His time.

Twelve

God Calls Us to Wait

Patience is the companion of wisdom.

St. Augustine,
church father

Chinese bamboo is fascinating. To grow Chinese bamboo, you plant a seed. Then you water and fertilize it. At the end of the first year, nothing happens. During the second year, those nurturing the bamboo seeds continue to water and fertilize the soil, but still nothing happens. The third year, they water and fertilize the soil, with the same results. This pattern continues through the fourth year. It's not until the fifth year that, sometime during the ongoing watering and fertilizing, a shoot of bamboo will pierce the soil. In just six weeks, a Chinese bamboo tree will grow to nearly ninety feet tall.

How long does it take to grow Chinese bamboo ninety feet tall? Does it take six weeks? Or five years? The answer probably depends on your perspective. If you happened upon the seedlings during those thriving six weeks, you'd think the trees grew at an incredible rate. But if you were the one planting, watering, and fertilizing all those years, then you'd know just how much time it requires. You'd also know that if you hadn't applied all that water and fertilizer for all of those years, there wouldn't be a Chinese bamboo tree to enjoy.

In all of our lives, we have experiences like a Chinese bamboo tree. We may hope or expect God to do something quickly, instantly, or in our expected time frame, but God moves much more slowly. The work He is doing may take weeks, months, years, or even decades. Like anyone who has sat and watched the ground where Chinese bamboo tree seeds have been planted, we may be tempted to believe that God isn't doing anything at all. We don't see growth. We don't see movement. We don't see breakthrough. But when God finally responds, He exceeds all of our wildest hopes and expectations.

Patience and perseverance go together.

As followers of God, we are all called to wait. At times God will use the Scriptures to remind us of the importance of waiting on Him. Other times we'll find that the whispers to wait come in the form of sermons, life experiences, and circumstances. Yet God is faithful. He will do more than we ever imagine.

1. What is one thing in your life that you had to wait on for what felt like forever?

2. *What, for you, is the hardest part of waiting?*

3. *Have you ever had a time in your life when you felt that God wanted you to wait? What was the experience? What did you learn from it?*

Throughout the Scriptures when you see patience mentioned, you'll often discover the mention or idea of perseverance. Patience and perseverance go together.

4. *Read **Galatians 6:7–10**. According to this passage, how do patience and perseverance work together?*

5. *What kinds of situations cause you to become "weary while doing good" (v. 9)? What is the promise to those who persevere in this passage?*

6. *Read **James 5:7–8**. Why do you think that when the Scripture talks about waiting, it often draws on the images of farming the land?*

Though answering God's call to wait can be challenging, it's important to remember that God is patient with each of us. He is the One who exemplifies what it means to be patient.

7. *Look up the following passages. What does each one reveal about the patience of God?*

Exodus 34:6:

Romans 15:5:

1 Peter 3:20:

2 Peter 3:15:

8. *What opportunities is God giving you to grow in patience and learn to wait on Him in your own life right now?*

God often doesn't answer us in the way or within the time frame that we would like. This is a normal part of the spiritual journey, but we should take heart. If we remain faithful, we will have a story of God's goodness in our lives that we would not have any other way.

Digging Deeper

God is faithful to make sure we don't miss what He is trying to say to us. How do we know? Because God is the Good Shepherd. Just as a sheep is wired to respond to the voice of its shepherd, we are wired to respond to the voice of God in our lives. Read **John 10:1–16.** How do the sheep respond to the shepherd? What comfort do you find in knowing that God is your Shepherd? How has God revealed His shepherdlike care in your own life?

Bonus Activity

Plant an avocado seed:

1. *Soak the seed in hot water for half an hour.*

2. *Cut a small sliver off the pointed end of the seed.*

3. In a small pot, plant the seed in sandy soil, with the cut end slightly above the surface of the soil.

4. Place the pot in indirect sunlight, in a warm place.

5. Water as needed to keep the soil moist, but not soggy.

Look at your plant every day. Does it seem to be taking forever to sprout? Be patient, and each time you observe your plant, take the time to pray about something for which you've been seeking an answer for what seems like a long time. The answer will come. And your avocado? Don't worry. The seed will sprout by the end of a month. (If you need help with your seed, visit http://www.weekend gardener.net/plant-propagation/plant-avocado-seed-090909.htm.)

Leader's Guide

Chapter 1: God's Voice Creates

Focus: *With mere words God spoke our world and all its wonders into existence. When God speaks to you and me, He is speaking life, hope, and a future.*

1. *Gently encourage participants to share moments from their own lives when they've encountered God. Answers will differ. Some people may have encountered God at church or through music, while others will have encountered or heard from Him while spending time in nature or within the context of community.*

2. *Throughout the study, this question will be examined more in-depth, but take notes as participants share their immediate responses to this question. For participants who can't identify anything specific, encourage them that this is what this study is designed to help them with, and God is faithful. If we want to hear His voice, God will ensure that we don't miss a word.*

3. *Some participants may prefer to watch the solar systems being created while others would prefer to see the creatures of the deep being designed. Celebrate and affirm the unique perspectives of every participant.*

4. *Answers will vary, but one of the amazing things about the creation story is that it is a beautiful artistic display of God at work—creating order and wonder out of chaos and darkness. The creation story also reminds us of God's deep commitment to His people and our world. It reminds us that God is our Creator and*

He is the first one we should turn to in life—because He knows us better than anyone else.

5. *The commandment to keep the Sabbath refers to the creation story and God's choice to rest on the seventh day. Most of the other commandments don't offer any history or explanation, but it's as if God wants the people to know that He has designed a Sabbath, a day of rest, for them since the beginning of time.*

6. *God displayed His power through thunder and lightning, the sound of a trumpet and the sight of smoke. They heard, saw, and smelled God's presence. This left the people trembling with fear. Moses reminded the people not to be afraid, but they were aware of God's power and the seriousness of walking in obedience.*

7. *Answers:*

   Nehemiah 9:6: God made the heavens, the highest heavens, the seas, and the stars. God gives life to everything.

   Psalm 24:1–2: The earth and everything in it, including its inhabitants, are the Lord's. He founded the earth upon the seas.

   Psalm 33:6: The heavens were made by the word of the Lord; the stars, by God's breath.

8. *For many, knowing God's power and ability to create life with mere words makes us want to be more responsive to Him and the ways He speaks to us.*

Digging Deeper

The Bible describes everything that God made as "very good." We don't know exactly why the writer described it as very good, but it may signify a completeness or wholeness or perfection to the work

God had done. Some people struggle to look at themselves through God's eyes—recognizing that God has made them, and God does good work.

Chapter 2: God's Voice Invites

Focus: *God's voice invites us into a deeper relationship with Him through prayer. If we want to hear God's voice, then we need to take advantage of this golden opportunity to seek and know Him.*

1. *All of us are wired differently. For some, grabbing heaps of pebbles comes naturally, while others would prefer to grab only one or two. Fear, insecurities, and being uncomfortable with the situation may prevent us from laying hold of everything available.*

2. *Answers will vary. Some of us may be bold and brave with God and ask for everything that we can think of, while others may be more hesitant. We may ask for financial provision, health, relational healing, strength, grace, love, or so many other things.*

3. *Jesus was delivering the Sermon on the Mount when He instructed His followers to ask, seek, and knock with the promise that those who do so will be rewarded. He pointed to the nature of God as a good God. He wants to give good gifts to His children.*

4. *Answers:*

   Genesis 24:26: He bowed in order to pray to God.

Numbers 20:6: Moses and Aaron fell on their faces as they prayed.

1 Kings 8:22: Solomon stood with his hands spread out toward heaven.

1 Kings 8:54: Solomon had been kneeling with his hands spread out toward heaven.

5. *This passage reminds us that the Holy Spirit Himself intercedes or prays for us when we can't find the words. When we can only offer up aches and murmurs to God, He still hears us and prays to God on our behalf. That is an amazing truth!*

6. *Answers:*

Scripture Reference	What Is Being Asked for in the Prayer?
Genesis 18:23–26	Mercy on Sodom
Genesis 32:24–26	Blessing
Daniel 9:4–6, 17–19	Forgiveness for people
Matthew 6:11	Provision
Ephesians 3:14–19	Strength for the Ephesians

7. *Answers will vary. These passages challenge us to pray for others, forgive others, trust God for provision, and ask for His blessing on our lives, among other things.*

8. *Answers will vary.*

Digging Deeper

Humility is the ability to put our pride aside and come to God with open hearts. God promises to hear the prayers, forgive their sins, and heal their land. Answers will vary. For some this will be a new idea; others will have seen this work in their lives. Consider asking the participants if they have stories to share of this being true in their own lives.

Chapter 3: God's Voice Exposes

Focus: *When God's voice exposes something in our hearts, it's to bring us to wholeness in our relationship with Him and others—if we listen to Him.*

1. *This opening question is meant to be a fun conversation starter. Encourage all the women to participate in this group-friendly discussion question.*

2. *Answers will vary. Trying to figure out who did it is always enjoyable, but encourage participants to discuss the elements of a great detective story.*

3. *Cain was upset because his offering to God was not looked on with favor. He was angry, and his face was downcast. He probably felt jealousy and anger toward his brother.*

4. *The Lord asked, "Why are you angry? And why has your countenance fallen? If you do well, will you not be accepted? And if you do not do well, sin lies at the door. And its desire is for you, but you should rule over it." The Lord revealed that the darkness that came into Cain's heart was very dark indeed. He instructed him to choose righteousness. Instead, Cain killed his brother.*

5. *Answers will vary, but most of us have been in situations in our families and workplaces where we struggled with jealousy, anger, and unforgiveness. Encourage participants who are comfortable with sharing to share their own stories.*

6. *David was not allowed to build the temple because he was a warrior and had killed. Instead, Solomon was chosen.*

7. *David gave Solomon lots of practical instruction on building the temple, from the design of its buildings to the pattern for its storerooms to its inner rooms. He also instructed those who would serve in the temple, and told them exactly what materials they were to use in building the temple. But of all the instruction David gave to his son, the spiritual instruction was the most valuable. He reminded him that the Lord searches the heart and knows everything. Solomon was to be strong and courageous and do the work.*

8. *Answers will vary, but it's worth noting that when God speaks to us, there's often a timeliness to His words. He will reveal something we need to know in the moment or may need to know in the future for the work that God has for us to do.*

Digging Deeper

Answers will vary. Jesus' words in these chapters give instruction, joy, and hope. His words will surprise or encourage the participants in different ways.

Chapter 4: God's Voice Surprises

Focus: *When you're listening for God, you can expect the unexpected. God's voice has a way of surprising us and catching us off guard. God has more to say to you than you ever imagined.*

1. *Answers will vary, but throughout Scripture we find God calling people to do the impossible. Encourage participants to share their stories of times when they felt God's leading and responded in obedience, and other times when they did not.*

2. *Answers will vary.*

3. *Answer will vary, but both Eli and Samuel must have been surprised, since the passage begins by letting us know that in that time period the Word of the Lord was rare. Samuel said to God, "Speak, LORD, for your servant hears." Samuel wanted to hear from God and had a heart willing to respond in obedience.*

4. *In this amazing encounter, Isaiah had a vision and saw the Lord. The scene had a profound impact on him as he became aware of his own sinful nature and the fallenness of mankind. God asked Isaiah, "Whom shall I send?" and Isaiah's response was, "Here am I! Send me."*

5. *For some, Jesus invited them to follow Him and spend the day with Him. Peter was called by his brother to meet the Messiah. Jesus also just told men to follow Him, and the men obeyed, spread the Word, and believed.*

6. *Answers will vary. Some will have come to know Jesus because a family member OR friend introduced them. Others will have had profound spiritual experiences, like Nathaniel's.*

7. *Answers will vary. Encourage participants to share stories from their own encounters with Jesus through the Scriptures.*

8. *Answers will vary.*

Digging Deeper

Answers will vary. We don't know exactly why God met Jeremiah in this way, but through it God established Jeremiah as His prophet. God meets people in different ways. They experience God's voice in different expressions. God may have spoken to you through a sermon, a song, Scripture, or even a dream. Others may encounter God differently. But God is faithful to make Himself real to us and confirm what He is saying through the Scriptures.

Chapter 5: God's Word as Foundation and Filter

Focus: *God's Word helps us discern whether or not what we're hearing is truly from God. By becoming familiar with Scripture, we are more equipped to detect God's voice in our lives.*

Bible Trivia Quick Quiz Answers: 1-c, 2-b, 3-c, 4-b, 5-a, 6-c, 7-b, 8-a, 9-a, 10-b

1. *Answers will vary. Participants are all at different levels of understanding and reading Scripture. While some may read the Bible every day, others may never have. Encourage the participants to consider reading the Bible as part of their daily time with God.*

2. *While some participants may enjoy reading the Bible, others may struggle with reading and studying it.*

3. *The devil saw that Jesus was hungry and tempted Him by telling Him to turn the rocks into food. Jesus replied by quoting Deuteronomy 8:3.*

4. *The devil tried to convince Jesus to throw Himself off of the temple roof. Jesus said no by quoting Deuteronomy 6:16. The devil misused Scripture in this passage. Jesus corrected him by reciting other Scripture contradicting the verse the devil used.*

5. *The devil offered the whole kingdom if Jesus would bow down to him. Jesus quoted Deuteronomy 6:13, saying that He was to worship the Lord alone. Jesus could have easily succumbed to the temptation of the devil. The devil even used Scripture to disguise his evil plan. However, since Jesus understood the Scriptures, He knew better than to believe the devil's words.*

6. *Answers:*

Scripture Reference	What Is Revealed about God's Word?
Psalm 119:89	God's Word is eternal.
Isaiah 40:8	God's Word stands forever.
Matthew 5:18	Nothing will disappear from God's Word.
Psalm 119:11	God's Word is to be used and remembered so we won't sin against God.

7. *Answers will vary. Often when we remember God's Word, we are able to listen to what He would say in a situation, causing us to change our original direction or decision.*

8. *God's Word is filled only with truth. If something we hear does not line up with Scripture, it cannot be from God.*

Digging Deeper

Answers will vary, but have some of the participants share examples of seeing God's Word used in their lives.

Chapter 6: God's Colorful Expressions

Focus: *God reveals Himself in colorful ways throughout the Scriptures and in our lives through His Spirit.*

1. *Answers will vary. Encourage participants to share times when God spoke to them in surprising or colorful ways.*

2. *Answers will vary.*

3. *Answers will vary. This question is designed to help participants consider new ways God may want to speak to them.*

4. *God is creative, all-powerful, and all-knowing. Throughout Scripture He spoke to people in different ways, reminding us that each of us is unique and our relationship with God is unique. God chose a burning bush to meet with Moses and an angel in the middle of the night to meet with Jacob.*

5. *God's thoughts are completely different. They have a higher meaning and come from a different vantage point or perspective that we do not have.*

6. *God's Spirit reveals God and His wisdom to us.*

7. *Answers will vary, but God knows everything, and He has plans for our lives that are greater than anything we can imagine. Sometimes waiting for God to reveal Himself is hard. It requires patience, persistence in prayer, and trusting God. Yet 1 Corinthians 2 reminds us that He is faithful.*

8. *Answers will vary. Encourage participants to persist in prayer, and gently remind them that there are some things God does not answer right away or even in this lifetime.*

Digging Deeper

God's voice sounded like a trumpet in this passage. Sometimes God is loud and clear, like a trumpet, and other times He is more difficult to recognize and it is harder to discern what He is communicating.

Chapter 7: God's Personal Touch

Focus: *Sometimes God makes Himself real in ways we don't even expect—but that are highly personal and incredibly meaningful to us.*

1. *Answers will vary. God uses amazing people and ways to communicate His love and faithfulness to us in difficult situations.*

2. *Answers will vary, but this question should encourage some fun discussion and remembering God's faithfulness.*

3. *God longs for a personal relationship with each of us. Just as no two of your personal relationships look exactly alike, our relationships with God will look different too.*

4. *Stephen explained why Jesus is the Messiah, the Promised One, and explained it in terms of the fulfillment of the Old Testament. In response, the people were angry and stoned him. Stephen responded by asking God for their forgiveness.*

5. *Saul was there and gave approval to Stephen's death.*

6. *Answers will vary, but it's interesting to see just how profound the encounter was for Saul. He encountered a light from heaven, a voice, and blindness. He was undergoing a profound transformation in his spiritual life. Once his eyes were opened, he would see things differently.*

7. *Answers will vary, but God included Ananias in the healing of Saul—the restoration of his eyesight. It's interesting to note that after he was healed, he spent several days with the disciples in Damascus. He built relationships. He became part of the Christian community.*

8. *Answers will vary, but God often uses others to speak into our lives.*

Digging Deeper

Answers will vary, but the psalmist was waiting in expectation that God would answer. This is important, because when we are expectant for God to answer, we look for Him and we live with our eyes and hearts open for all He wants to do.

Chapter 8: God Whispers

Focus: *God wants to speak to us. He desires a relationship with us. God often gets our attention with subtle nudges.*

1. *God was revealing something about His nature to Elijah. In 1 Kings 18, God had displayed His power in the form of fire on top of Mount Carmel. Now He is revealing Himself to Elijah in a whole new way.*

2. *Elijah probably listened for God in the midst of the noisy wind, earthquake, and fire. When Elijah didn't hear God in those things, his heart was willing, ready, and able to hear.*

3. *All of us have had times when we are overwhelmed by fear, loss, and discouragement. Gently encourage participants who feel comfortable to share from their own life stories.*

4. *It's encouraging to hear what God uses during our most difficult times to encourage us and remind us of His love.*

5. *Answers will vary.*

6. *God instructed Elijah on where to go physically. Then He instructed him to anoint a new king over Aram, a new king over Israel, and a new prophet who would follow after Elijah. He also reminded*

Elijah that he was not alone—seven thousand others had not bowed the knee to Baal.

7. *Answers:*

   Spiritually: God sent the angel to feed and instruct Elijah. God spoke to Elijah and met him in a profound way.

   Physically: God provided food for Elijah and gave him the strength to travel to Horeb.

   Emotionally: God reminded Elijah that he was not alone, and gave him hope.

   Relationally: God was about to give Elijah a new friend, Elisha, and remind him that he was not the only one who was faithful in Israel—there were many more.

8. *Answers will vary. We all have different spiritual, physical, emotional, and relational needs, and God meets them all in different ways. Encourage a few participants to share the ways in which God has met their needs.*

Digging Deeper

Answers will vary. Little is known about Enoch. Genesis 5:18–24 describes his life. We know that he walked with God and was no more. We know Enoch had a special relationship with God compared to all the others listed in Genesis 5. Faith is essential to all of our faith journeys. We have to choose to trust God—even when those around us do not.

Chapter 9: God Calls Us to Know and Love Him

Focus: *God invites us into a personal relationship with Him where we can grow in our faith. God loves us and calls us to love Him and express that love by loving others.*

1. *Answers will vary. Encourage participants to share things they may have learned or experienced from a seminar, weekend retreat, or road trip where they had time to focus on God.*

2. *Answers will vary. Batterson's observation is simple but profound. We may be tempted to try to work for God or get work done for God, but ultimately God is the foundation for everything we do—including any work that takes place. When we ground ourselves in God, it changes our attitude and actions.*

3. *Some participants will find it easier to simply do things for God, while others will find it easier to reflect on all that God has done for them. They go hand in hand.*

4. *The church was commended for its deeds, hard work, perseverance, intolerance of the wicked, endurance, and readiness to test teachers to see if they were true. They also didn't like the practices of the Nicolaitans, which God Himself hated. They were challenged because they had forgotten their first love. They were told that they needed to return and do the things they did in the beginning of their faith journeys.*

5. *Encourage participants to reflect on when they first came to know Jesus. Be sensitive to those who are new to knowing God or in the journey of getting to know Him more.*

6. *Answers will vary. Our love for God is meant to mature and grow in depth and commitment. All of us experience times when our love for God wanes. We need to be intentional about fanning the flames of our love of God.*

7. *Answers will vary, but most of us feel the pressure and heat that comes with being a jar of clay. We know God is doing something amazing in us. After all, He is the Master Potter. But we don't get to see all that He is doing or all the glory He is bringing to Himself through us.*

8. *Some may choose to read the Bible more or be more intentional about prayer. Others may recognize the need to attend a church or Bible study. Others may recognize the need to offer up more thanks for all God is doing in their lives. Still others may recognize that their love for God comes alive when they're serving or singing or creating art.*

Digging Deeper

The psalmist called people to sing for joy and shout loudly to God. We're invited to offer up our thanks and kneel before Him, and we're reminded of His power and strength. The psalmist challenges us not to allow our hearts to grow hard, like the Israelites who wandered in the desert for forty years. We need to stay tender and responsive to God. Answers will vary. Allow the participants to share as they feel comfortable.

Chapter 10: God Calls Us to Obedience

Focus: *God doesn't just invite us to know Him and love Him. We are also meant to obey Him as an expression of knowing and loving Him. Obedience is one of the greatest calls of God we can respond to in our lives.*

1. *Answers will vary, but everyone has experienced a time when they felt they shouldn't do something and did it anyway. Sometimes when we disobey, we don't recognize the damage we cause to our relationships, our finances, our health, or other aspects of our lives.*

2. *We may try to tell ourselves that it's not really God, it's not really that important, or it's no big deal. We can be highly creative when it comes to justifying doing our own thing.*

3. *Samuel instructed Saul to attack and completely destroy everything that belonged to the Amalekites. Nothing was to be spared among the people or their animals.*

4. *Saul attacked the Amalekites and destroyed the people, but he took their king, Agag, alive. He also spared the best of the sheep and cattle, the fat calves, the lambs, and everything that was good. Saul was willing to destroy what was worthless, but not what was valuable in his eyes. In the process, he disobeyed what Samuel had commanded as a prophet of God.*

5. *Most of us find partial disobedience more tempting because it's easier to rationalize. We can justify obeying God in part as long as we don't wholly disobey Him.*

6. Saul blessed Samuel and claimed to have carried out the Lord's instructions. Samuel commented that he could hear the bleating of sheep and the sound of cattle.

7. Saul tried to argue that he spared the best sheep and cattle for the Lord. He contended that he had fulfilled the mission God gave him, and the only reason he had spared the animals was to give them up as an offering.

8. Samuel told the king that obedience is better than sacrifice. By choosing not to obey, Saul was walking in rebellion and arrogance and was rejecting the Word of God. As a result, He lost the throne.

Digging Deeper

God gave the people over to the stubbornness of their own hearts. God longs for us to obey Him because His laws and instruction lead each of us into the best possible life—one that honors Him.

Chapter 11: God Calls Us to Faith

Focus: *God invites us to trust Him wholly and choose to walk by faith. At times, we may be tempted to forget just how important faith is to our spiritual journeys, but it's essential to following God.*

1. Answers will vary.

2. Prayer, studying the Scriptures, spending time with wiser and older followers of Jesus, worship, and solitude are just a few of the ways that we can be challenged and sharpened in our spiritual journeys.

3. *Jesus was asking them to do something—forgive—that they knew they could not do on their own. Whenever God asks us to do something we cannot do on our own, we are asked to trust, believe, and grow in faith.*

4. *Answers*

Pieces of Armor	Represents
Belt	Truth
Breastplate	Righteousness
Shoes	Readiness and Peace
Shield	Faith
Helmet	Salvation
Sword	Spirit—Word of God

5. *The shield of faith helps us extinguish the flaming arrows of the evil one. Trusting in God means that we aren't trusting in that which isn't true. It protects us, guards us, and helps us choose the best possible life.*

6. *Jesus reminded them that He doesn't do anything He doesn't see His Father doing. He told them that God was going to reveal greater miracles than healings—He was also going to raise some from the dead. He challenged them not to judge Him but to remember that God judges all people. And whoever honors Jesus honors God.*

7. *Jesus promises eternal life to those who believe in Him. Gently encourage participants to share why they have or have not chosen to accept this promise.*

8. *Answers will vary.*

Digging Deeper

Answers will vary, but Jesus was teaching His disciples the power of faith. It can do far more than we can expect or imagine. God invites us to live by faith, to trust Him with everything, and to serve Him with everything we've got.

Chapter 12: God Calls Us to Wait

Focus: *God often doesn't answer us in the way or within the time frame that we would like. This is a normal part of the spiritual journey, but we should take heart. If we remain faithful, we will each have a story of God's goodness in our lives that we would not have any other way.*

1. *Participants may have had to wait to get married, have or adopt a child, earn a high school diploma or college degree, buy a house, get a job, be healed from a disease or sickness, recover from an accident, or many more things.*

2. *Waiting challenges each of us in different ways. It challenges us to trust God, remain faithful, grow in patience, learn to persevere, and much more.*

3. *Encourage participants to share personal stories from their own lives.*

4. *We are encouraged not to grow weary in doing good. We are to be patient and persevere. Our efforts will be rewarded with a rich harvest.*

5. *We may find ourselves tiring of doing good in our workplaces, homes, families, or communities, but we're encouraged to persevere. God is faithful.*

6. *Farmers know firsthand that you cannot place a seed in the soil today and cash in on a harvest tomorrow. They have to prepare the soil, plant, nurture the seeds and land, water, fertilize, and wait until the harvest comes.*

7. *Answers:*

   Exodus 34:6: God is slow to anger.

   Romans 15:5: God gives endurance and encouragement.

   1 Peter 3:20: God waited patiently while Noah built the ark.

   2 Peter 3:15: God's patience means salvation.

8. *Answers will vary.*

Digging Deeper

The sheep hear the shepherd's voice and respond. They will not respond to the voice of a stranger. The sheep know their shepherd. Answers will vary. Consider reflecting on Psalm 23 and all the ways God is intimately involved in our lives as He leads, guides, restores, anoints, and calls us.

Notes

Chapter 3

1. www.spymuseum.org.

Chapter 7

1. Glen Van Ekeren, *Speaker's Sourcebook II* (New York: Prentice Hall, 1994), 327.

Chapter 9

1. Adapted from Mark Batterson, *Primal: A Quest for the Lost Soul of Christianity* (Colorado Springs: Multnomah), 155–56.

Chapter 11

1. Adapted from http://www.jesussite.com/illustrations/living.html.

About the Author

A popular speaker at churches and leading conferences such as Catalyst and Thrive, Margaret Feinberg was recently named one of the '30 Emerging Voices' who will help lead the church in the next decade by *Charisma* magazine and one of the '40 Under 40' who will shape Christian publishing by Christian Retailing, she has written more than two dozen books and Bible studies including the critically-acclaimed *The Organic God, The Sacred Echo, Scouting the Divine* (Zondervan) and their corresponding DVD Bible studies. She is known for her relational teaching style and inviting people to discover the relevance of God and His Word in a modern world.

Margaret and her books have been covered by national media including: CNN, the Associated Press, *Los Angeles Times, Dallas Morning News, Washington Post, Chicago Tribune, Newsday, Houston Chronicle, Beliefnet.com, Salon.com, USATODAY.com, MSNBC.com, RealClearPolitics.com, Forbes.com,* and many others.

About the Author

Margaret currently lives in Morrison, Colorado, with her 6'8" husband, Leif. When she's not writing or traveling, she enjoys anything outdoors, lots of laughter, and their superpup, Hershey. But she says some of her best moments are spent communicating with her readers. So go ahead, drop her a note:

Margaret Feinberg

PO Box 441

Morrison, CO 80465

www.margaretfeinberg.com
info@margaretfeinberg.com

Become a fan on Facebook
Follow on twitter: @mafeinberg

Additional Resources

What Shall We Study Next?

Women of Faith® has numerous study guides available
that will draw you closer to God.

Visit www.womenoffaith.com or www.thomasnelson.com
for more information.

Discovering God in Your Creativity
You Are Made in the Image of a Creative God

*In the beginning God created the
heavens and the earth.*

GENESIS 1:1

The initial splash of creativity is displayed in the first words of the Bible: "In the beginning God created. . . ." With those words, God took the plunge into designing the cosmos and the earth. As the first chapters of Genesis reveal, God did not hold back! He created a spectrum of colors, tastes, smells, and sounds.

Today we still enjoy the bounty of all God has made and formed. If you're an early riser, then you know the sunrise is a work of art in and of itself. Some mornings it looks as if God has finger-painted the sky. For those who prefer to sleep in, God makes sure you don't miss His handiwork either, as sunsets reveal colors unimaginable. With vibrant hues of fuchsias, olives, and cerulean blues, God's color spectrum far exceeds that of a Crayola 164-Pack.

This study is designed to douse you in the creativity of God as if it were a cool spring on a hot summer day. My hope is that you'll decide to make time to pull off your shoes and experience the delight that comes with trying something new and unexpected. You may just find yourself refreshed and rejuvenated in ways you never imagined!

We live in a world where we're constantly pressed with demands on every side—from our work, our home, and our families. While many of those requirements are good, if they stack up too high, they can squeeze the life and the creativity out of us. We can become too busy and even too exhausted to engage in our creative pursuits. But that was never what God intended. God wants us to think creatively and express our love for Him and others creatively.

My hope and prayer is that through this study you will once again become awestruck by the Creator of the universe and all He has done and is continuing to do through your life. May you unlock your inner creativity in such a way that it makes a tangible difference, not only in your life, but also in the lives of those around you.

Blessings,

Margaret Feinberg

Experiencing Peace
With God, You Can Live Beyond Fear

The Lord gives strength to his people; the
Lord blesses his people with peace.

PSALM 29:11, NIV

Have you ever had something totally rock your world? You're going through life with sunny skies and smooth sailing when, seemingly out of nowhere, you're hit with a storm that takes your breath away. Just minutes before you were quiet, calm, and collected, but now you wonder, *What happened? Am I going to lose everything? What's going to save me this time?*

The truth is, becoming a follower of Jesus doesn't make all the storms of life head in the opposite direction. Sometimes they'll still blow our way. But when those storms come, we find ourselves clinging to an anchor, tucked away inside a cove, and safely harbored in the arms of God. God never intended us to live in fear. He designed us to walk in faith. Even as we're making that journey, we'll still encounter challenges, trials, and difficult times. How do we face them? By embracing the peace of God.

When the Bible talks about peace, it usually refers to one of two types of peace: peace *with* God and the peace *of* God. Peace with God means through grace and the wondrous work Jesus did on the cross we can experience peace with God. But that's not all! We also get to enjoy the peace of God. Throughout the Scriptures we are reminded that we don't need to be anxious for a single thing. We can choose to trust God, pray, be thankful, and enjoy the contentment that comes with knowing God has everything under control. That doesn't mean that the peace of God is always easy to recognize according to outward circumstances. In fact, sometimes when things look their roughest and toughest on the outside, peace can reign on the inside. That's good news because it means the peace of God is not dependent on outward activity or happenstance.

By placing our trust in the Prince of Peace, we receive a peace that surpasses our wildest imaginations. My hope is that as you go through this study, you will fully embrace the peace that God gives you as His child.

Blessings,

Margaret Feinberg

Get Fresh...

nthusiasm, Inspiration, Strength
a **Women of Faith** weekend event!

Women of Faith, thousands of women come together for two days to laugh, cry, ship, share, and draw strength from each other and from God. Messages, music, more combine for a one-of-a-kind event designed by women for women.

"I'm always energized for months after attending these events!" –Angie G.

us at an event near you!

details and sign up at **womenoffaith.com** or call 888-49-FAITH (888-493-2484).

"God's presence was felt the very first moment we walked in the door and never left!" –Kellye H.

't Wait! Seats are Going Fast.

g your friends, bring your family, or just bring yourself . . . but whatever do, don't miss this opportunity. Register today!

WOMEN OF FAITH®

womenoffaith.com | 888.49.FAITH (888.493.2484)

Follow us on **facebook** **twitter**

Women of Faith events are productions of Thomas Nelson Live Events.